# MISSION
# LONDON

Author: Catherine Aragon
Designer: Nada Orlić

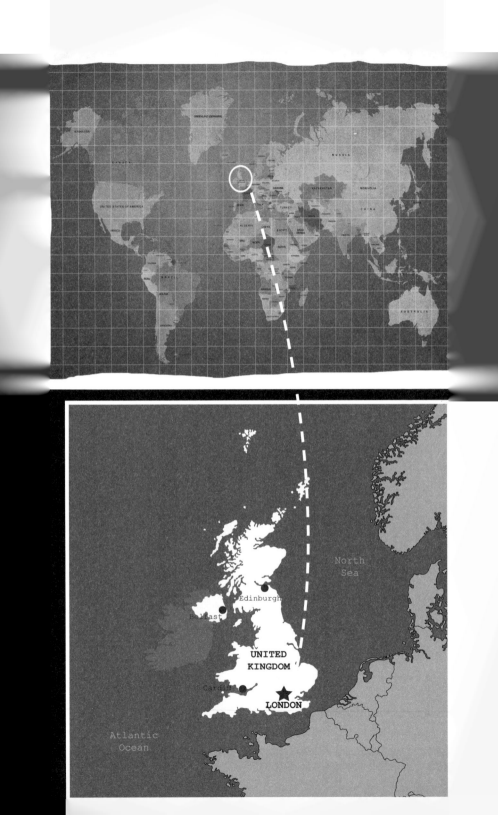

# CONTENTS

AFTER COMPLETING EACH MISSION, CHECK (√) THE BOX AND WRITE THE NUMBER OF POINTS EARNED.

AT THE END, WRITE THE TOTAL NUMBER OF POINTS HERE: ☐

# ATTENTION: FUTURE SPECIAL AGENTS <u>YOU</u> AND <u>CASE OFFICERS</u> <u>GROWNUPS</u>

## CONGRATULATIONS! THE SIA (SECRET INTERNATIONAL AGENCY) HAS SELECTED YOU AS A CANDIDATE TO BECOME A SPECIAL AGENT.

The SIA carries out important assignments, secretly collecting intelligence in all corners of the globe. ("Intelligence" is spy-speak for "information.") Currently, we are in dire need of agents. Many want to join us, but only a few have what it takes.

**HOW WILL YOU PROVE YOU'RE READY TO JOIN THE MOST ELITE SPY AGENCY IN THE WORLD?** You must complete a series of missions in London. Similar to a scavenger hunt (only better), these missions will require you to carry out challenging investigations and collect valuable intel (short for "intelligence"). For each mission, you'll earn points towards becoming a special agent.

**YOUR ASSIGNMENT: TRAVEL TO LONDON WITH YOUR TEAM, LED BY YOUR CASE OFFICER.** (A case officer accompanies agents on missions. Your case officer is your parent or other trusted adult.) You must earn at least 100 points to become a SIA special agent.

-The list of missions and scorecard are on page 1.

-Read the "Anytime Missions" early, so that you'll remain on alert and ready to earn points. You can complete these at any time.

-You don't need to complete all of the missions to reach 100 points or complete them in any particular order.

# BONUS MISSION

Want even more London fun? Visit **scavengerhuntadventures.com/bonus** (all lowercase) today to download your **free bonus mission: "The Center of London."**

(Plus, you'll get *The Museum Spy*, our free e-book!)

"Get Your Bonus Mission Today!"

# MISSION RULES

- Be kind and respectful to team members.

- Your case officer (your parent or other trusted adult) has the final decision regarding point awards.

- Your case officer serves as the official "scorekeeper."

- Your case officer has the final decision on what missions will be attempted. (Don't worry, you can still earn enough points to become an agent without completing all the missions.)

- Always be on alert. You never know when a chance to earn points lies just around the corner.

**TO CONCEAL THEIR REAL IDENTITIES, SPECIAL AGENTS ALWAYS USE CODE NAMES. FOR EXAMPLE, JAMES BOND'S CODE NAME IS 007. THINK OF YOUR OWN CODE NAME TO USE DURING YOUR MISSION IN LONDON.**

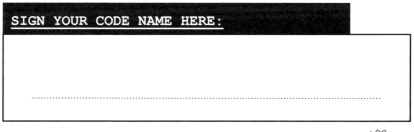

**SIGN YOUR CODE NAME HERE:**

DATE

**IMPORTANT: FOR THE MISSIONS YOU'LL NEED A PEN/ PENCIL AND A CAMERA.**

LET THE MISSIONS BEGIN — GOOD LUCK!

# WESTMINSTER ABBEY

**SPECIAL AGENTS ALWAYS NEED TO HAVE THEIR EYES PEELED FOR INTELLIGENCE: CLUES AND CRITICAL INFORMATION THAT OTHERS OFTEN MISS. CAN YOU FIND THE 'INTEL' NEEDED TO COMPLETE THIS MISSION?**

For almost 1000 years England's royals have been crowned, married, and buried at this very location. This mission is chock-full of clues, waste no time, let's get to work.

## *Exterior*

☐ FIND GARGOYLES WITH THEIR TONGUES STICKING OUT.

**2 POINTS**

**52**

TOTAL POINTS

- GARGOYLES
- ST. PETER'S STATUE & PAINTING
- COMPLEX DESIGNS
- ROYAL TOMBS & MODELS
- SKELETON
- UNKNOWN WARRIOR

- CORONATION CHAIR
- NEWTON'S MONUMENT
- LAST SUPPER MOSAIC
- ELIZABETH I MONUMENT
- MARY STUART MONUMENT
- RAF CHAPEL
- SHAKESPEARE STATUE

**2 POINTS**

☐ TRACK DOWN THE STATUE OF SAINT* PETER, HOLDING A CROSS AND KEYS (THE KEYS TO HEAVEN).

Saint Peter

**3 POINTS**

☐ BONUS: ONCE INSIDE, VENTURE TO THE ABBEY MUSEUM AND FIND THE REMAINS OF A PAINTING FROM THE 13TH CENTURY OF PETER WITH HIS KEYS.

*Saint = someone officially recognized by the church for his/her holiness and good works

5

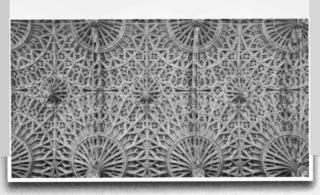

## *Interior*

☐ **TRACK DOWN THESE TWO COMPLEX DESIGNS.** **2 POINTS**

Hint: Keep a look out above your head and beneath your feet.

**The first (above):** part of a structure called "a wonder of the world," upon its completion in the 1500's. When you find it, imagine the time it would take to carve and construct this without the use of today's power tools.

**The second (below):** Part of an Italian job called the Cosmati Pavement dating from the 1200's, it originally contained Latin inscriptions that time has worn away. (Latin was the language of Ancient Rome.) One of the inscriptions foretold the world lasting for exactly 19,683 years.

**This black-and-white illustration provides only a small piece of the overall design. If you manage to track down the Cosmati Pavement then you definitely have the keen eyes necessary for a secret agent.**

Throughout the Abbey lie eerie reminders of England's deceased royals. Hundreds of years ago, following the death of a royal, wooden and wax models, complete with real hair, face paint, and clothing were used for funerals and afterwards

would sometimes even rest beside gravestones. These models were a bit better looking (and smelling) than the royals' dead bodies. You can also uncover tombs with life-like sculptures resting-in-peace on top.

**HUNT DOWN A ROYAL:**

☐ **LYING SIDE-BY-SIDE ATOP A TOMB WITH HIS/ HER SPOUSE**

☐ **WITH ONLY HIS/HER HEAD REMAINING**

☐ **WITH AN ANIMAL**

☐ **LOUNGING ON HIS/HER SIDE**

☐ **WITH HIS/HER HANDS JOINED IN PRAYER**
(10 POINTS MAX)

Find the skeleton who has emerged from below to scare some helpless statues.

☐ **WHAT IS THE SKELETON AIMING TOWARDS THESE STATUES?**

2
POINTS

Hint: The skeleton awaits in St. Michael's Chapel.

Coronation Chair

Locate the Tomb of the Unknown Warrior, a shrine to those who gave their lives in war.

☐ **READ THE INSCRIPTION - WHAT DATE WAS THE SOLDIER BURIED HERE?**

**2** POINTS

☐ **TRACK DOWN THE CORONATION CHAIR.**

**2** POINTS

Don't even think about trying to take a break and relaxing in this chair. It's reserved strictly for royal tushies during their coronation\*. For over 700 years (since 1308), almost every single English monarch has received his or her crown while seated in this chair.

☐ **WHAT KIND OF ANIMAL SUPPORTS THE CHAIR?**

**1** POINT

☐ **WHO WAS THE MOST RECENT ROYAL TO BE CROWNED IN WESTMINSTER ABBEY?**

**1** POINT

Check with your case officer to obtain this piece of intelligence.

---

\*Coronation = a ceremony where a crown is placed on the head of a new king or queen

Isaac Newton

Hunt down the monument to Isaac Newton, the super-smart scientist and author who not only gave us the laws of gravity and motion, but also the ever-challenging subject of calculus.

☐ ON WHAT ITEMS DOES NEWTON'S ELBOW REST?

**2** POINTS

☐ BONUS: FIND ANOTHER FIGURE WHOSE ELBOW RESTS ON THE SAME KIND OF ITEM.

*1* POINT

☐ LOCATE A TELESCOPE SOMEWHERE ON HIS MONUMENT.

*2* POINTS

☐ FIND THE MOSAIC\* OF CHRIST'S GOLDEN CUP.

**2** POINTS

(Hint: Look for the larger mosaic of the Last Supper.)

\*Mosaic = a design made from tiny pieces of glass or stone

☐ UNCOVER THE INSCRIPTION NEAR THE MOSAIC: "THE KINGDOMS OF THIS WORLD ARE BECOME THE KINGDOMS OF OUR LORD AND OF HIS CHRIST."

*1* POINT

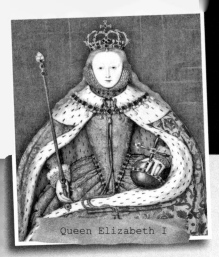

Queen Elizabeth I

The Queen's Symbol

☐ **HUNT DOWN THE MONUMENT TO QUEEN ELIZABETH I.**

2

This queen finds herself near the top of many "England's best queens" lists - under her rule in the 1500's the nation became more powerful as it defeated its arch enemy, Spain.

☐ **FIND HER SYMBOL: A UNICORN.**

POINT

(also a symbol of Scotland)

A Corset

☐ **LOCATE ELIZABETH'S CORSET.**

POINT

(Hint: It may be in the Abbey's museum.)

To imagine what it was like wearing a corset, suck in your stomach as much as you can. Imagine trying to maintain a clear head and make decisions involving the fate of an entire country or perhaps the world. To get an idea how Elizabeth (and any other poor woman who wore a corset) must have felt...

☐ **SUCK IN YOUR STOMACH AS FAR AS YOU CAN AND READ THE QUOTE ON THE NEXT PAGE, WHILE APPEARING AS SERIOUS AS POSSIBLE.**

3 POINTS

Your case officer will decide if you do a good job.

(Quote Note: VIII=8, VII=7, IV=4)

*"To the eternal memory of Elizabeth queen of England, France and Ireland, daughter of King Henry VIII, granddaughter of King Henry VII, great-grand-daughter to King Edward IV."*

☐ **UNCOVER THE ABOVE SENTENCE INSCRIBED IN LATIN SOMEWHERE ON ELIZABETH'S TOMB.**

Hint: Look for the countries of England, France, and Ireland in Latin (Angliae, Franciae, Hiberniae).

☐ **TRACK DOWN THE RED LION PERCHED AT THE FEET OF A NEARBY TOMB.**

This lion, the symbol of Scotland, guards the tomb of Mary, Queen of Scots. She and Elizabeth have quite a story.

my notes:

_____

_____

Hardly a day went by that Elizabeth wasn't looking over her shoulder, on guard against enemies(and so-called friends) seeking to overthrow or assassinate her. **Elizabeth had her eyes on this woman, Mary Queen of Scots.** Also known as Mary Stuart, this ambitious woman believed she could lay claim to Elizabeth's throne, thanks to her family history. She had already ruled over Scotland and France. (**She became Queen of Scotland at the ripe old age of six *days* old** because her father, the King of Scotland, died shortly after she was born.) For safekeeping, **Elizabeth had Mary locked up.**

Mary Queen of Scots

Queen Elizabeth

**A man by the name of Francis Walsingham served as Elizabeth's cunning spymaster.** Walsingham dispatched an agent to dig up proof that Mary was plotting to overthrow Elizabeth. **Walsingham's spy got a hold of encoded messages** secretly sent between Mary and her supporters **outlining a plan to do away with the queen.** Walsingham decoded the encrypted* messages and showed them to Elizabeth. Even though some questions remain as to whether Mary was truly behind the plot, Mary was sentenced to death by beheading.

Francis Walsingham

*Encrypted = written in a secret code

Shakespeare

On the lookout for enemy planes over London

Make your way to the Royal Air Force Chapel, whose stained glass window honors the RAF members who fought in World War II. The British, together with other Allied* powers, battled the Axis* powers. During the Battle of Britain, the city of London came under attack as warplanes of the evil Nazis bombed the city in the fall of 1940. Thanks to the bravery of the RAF and Allied airmen, even though the Germans (the Nazis) had more planes and pilots, the British managed to win, thereby preventing the Nazis from controlling Great Britain and winning the war.

*During World War II, the "Allies" (led by Great Britain, France, the U.S., China, and Russia) battled the "Axis" (led by Germany, Japan, and Italy).

☐ **TRACK DOWN THIS DESIGN, PART OF THE SYMBOL OF THE RAF 41ST SQUADRON\*.**

**2 POINTS**

A pilot in this squadron*, Eric Lock, was the RAF's "ace" in the sky. Even though he was wounded in battle, he still managed to take out 16 German planes, in keeping with the squadron's motto of "seek and destroy."

*Squadron = a military unit

Find the life-size statue of one of history's greatest writers, the playwright William Shakespeare. Even though he lived over 400 years ago, theatres around the world still perform his plays today. Upon this statue are words from one of his works, *The Tempest*.

☐ **WHAT WORD (BEGINNING WITH "T") IS HIS FINGER POINTING TO?**

**2 POINTS**

☐ **HOW MANY BOOKS REST BENEATH HIS ELBOW?**

**2 POINTS**

# PARLIAMENT & BIG BEN

Although this place is also called the Palace of Westminster, you won't find any royals living here. Instead it's home to the UK* Parliament – the House of Lords and House of Commons (similar to the Senate and House of Representatives in the U.S.). Next to this massive 1,000+ room structure, London's world-famous Big Ben towers over the Thames ("Tems").

Find this statue, with the statue's name inscribed on its base.

☐ **WHO IS IT?**

**2 POINTS**

*The "UK" includes England, Scotland, Wales, and Northern Ireland. "Great Britain" includes England, Scotland, and Wales.

14

This man ruled England from 1653-1658, during a short period of time when the monarchy had been abolished. He played a key role in getting the King of England, Charles I, executed. **This would come back to haunt him...from the grave.** Soon after the man's death (we'll call the man "X"), the monarchy returned to power, and Charles II (the son of Charles I), had a bone to pick with X. X's corpse had been resting peacefully at Westminster Abbey until the anniversary of the beheading of Charles I rolled around. Under orders from the Parliament of Charles II, X's corpse was dug up, hung from the gallows and beheaded. Some say the head was then displayed on a stick for around 25 years. Then, the stick snapped during a storm, and X's head fell to the ground. **No one knows for sure what really happened to the head,** as fakes popped up all over England. However, most accounts confirm that finally, in the 1960's, X's head was laid to rest in his college town of Cambridge.

X

Charles I

Charles II

After finding this statue, turn with your back towards the Palace of Westminster and head to the right – down St. Margaret Street towards Parliament Square. Walk until you arrive at Bridge Street, with Big Ben on your right and Parliament Square on your left. Scan the surrounding area to the left and hunt down the red telephone booths.

☐ **HAVE YOUR PHOTO TAKEN BESIDE ONE WITH BIG BEN IN THE BACKGROUND.**    **2 POINTS**

☐ **EXAMINE BIG BEN'S FACE AND ENSURE YOUR CLOCK IS SET TO BEN'S OFFICIAL TIME.**    **2 POINTS**

(Big Ben is actually the name of one of the bells inside the clock, but many people call the clock Big Ben.)

MI6 HQ

Just arrived in London or have you been here a few days? Either way, chances are, **without even realizing it, you've strolled by a handful of secret sites used by spies carrying out covert operations.** London, together with spy hubs like Washington, D.C. and Vienna, Austria, compete for the title of "**Spy Capital of the World.**" Just down the Thames (Thames = "Tems") River from Big Ben lies the international headquarters of **MI6 (Military Intelligence, Section 6) the UK's Secret Intelligence Service, a spy hotbed,** and home of the most famous agent of them all: James Bond.

James Bond

James Bond exists in the made-up world of movies and books - he probably wouldn't make it in the real world of secret agents. **The best spies are the ones you never ever suspect of spying in the first place.** Think back to the Londoners you've met: your hotel housekeeper, tour guide, or cab driver. Are they really as they appear…or **could they be a spy**? The same goes for those spy sites. The MI6 building doesn't attempt to hide its true purpose: the UK's spy headquarters. However, the next time you walk down a London sidewalk, glance around. Is the block filled with your run-of-the-mill office buildings, souvenir shops, and restaurants…or **could these really be spy sites in disguise**?

# BUCKINGHAM PALACE

*Changing of the Guard*

Buckingham Palace serves as the official HQ of the British monarch*. No false moves allowed here. The palace guards, members of the British military, have this place 100% secure. However, even Great

Britain's finest need a break. When it's time for the guards to go off-duty, new replacement soldiers arrive, complete with a formal military ceremony with music (a brass band), horses, and marching.

> *Monarch = someone (a king or queen) who rules a kingdom

The guards come from one of five units (listed on the next page). One way to tell them apart – the plume on the soldiers' black bearskin hats.

☐ **FROM WHAT REGIMENT(S) ARE THE GUARDS YOU SEE?**

**2 POINTS**

Grenadier Guards: White, worn on left side
Coldstream Guards: Red, worn on right side
Scots Guards: No plume
Irish Guards: Blue, worn on right side
Welsh Guards: Green and white, worn on left side

**FIND A SOLDIER WITH THIS INSIGNIA.**

☐ **THREE CHEVRONS (THE RANK OF SERGEANT)**

**1 POINT**

☐ **TWO CHEVRONS (THE RANK OF CORPORAL)**

**1 POINT**

☐ **BONUS: LOCATE A SOLDIER WHO'S SMILING.**

1 POINT

☐ **HUNT DOWN THIS STATUE OF ONE OF GREAT BRITAIN'S MOST FAMOUS QUEENS.**

2 POINTS

(part of a memorial to this royal, who became queen when she was only 18)

☐ **WHAT WAS HER NAME?**

1 POINT

Find it just above the words "Regina Imperatrix" ("Queen Empress" inscribed in Latin).

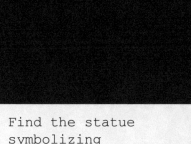

Find the statue symbolizing motherhood and charity (a mother with a group of children).

☐ **HOW MANY CHILDREN ARE WITH HER?**

`1 POINT`

Together with her husband, Prince Albert, this queen had more than a few children - she had nine. When Prince Albert died, she went into mourning and for the rest of her reign only appeared in black.

Prince Albert

Examine this photo of the queen.

☐ **DO YOU THINK THE SCULPTOR DID A GOOD JOB CREATING HER IMAGE?**

`1 POINT`

The Queen

# TRAFALGAR SQUARE

Admiral Nelson

At the ripe old age of 12, Horatio Nelson joined Great Britain's Royal Navy, a sea force forever at war with two other European powers yearning to rule the ocean blue: France and Spain. Nelson's swift skills in battle may have prevented the French from invading Great Britain, but **unfortunately he wasn't quick enough to dodge the deadly bullet of a French sniper at the Battle of Trafalgar, Spain** in 1805. Upon word of his tragic death, Great Britain began preparations for a grand funeral at St. Paul's Cathedral to honor this national hero. Back in Spain, attendants prepared Nelson's body for his four-week voyage back home in a manner fit for one of history's great sailors: **his corpse was placed in a casket filled with brandy,** a drink similar to wine (and later refilled with more wine) to keep it in tip-top shape.

☐ **FIND THE STATUE OF ADMIRAL NELSON.**

2 POINTS

**16**

TOTAL POINTS

☐ **LOCATE THIS RELIEF\* DEPICTING NELSON'S DEATH.**

**1 POINT**

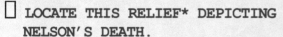

\*Relief = a flat sculpture

Nelson was one staunch seafarer. Even before the Battle of Trafalgar, he had lost sight in his right eye due to battle wounds. Then, he lost an arm while fighting the Spanish at the Battle of Santa Cruz. **A musket ball, a sort of large, old-fashioned bullet, hit him in the arm, and his injury was so life-threatening that the admiral's surgeon had to amputate.** Nelson endured the pain of amputation, but not even the pain of having his arm cut off was enough to keep him down. **In about an hour Nelson got off of the operating table and began sizing up the battle scene.** Examine Lord Nelson's statue.

☐ **WHICH ARM DID HE LOSE IN BATTLE?**

**1 POINT**

☐ **LIKE SO MANY TRAVELERS HAVE DONE BEFORE YOU, HAVE YOUR PHOTO SNAPPED WITH THE BRONZE LIONS.**

**2 POINTS**

23

☐ **WHAT U.S. PRESIDENT STANDS ON A LAWN BORDERING THE SQUARE*?**

This president, who led the U.S. to defeat their former colonial rulers, the British, vowed that he would never set foot on British soil again. The state of Virginia sent the dirt for the president's statue to stand upon, so that he could honor his vow.

*Hint: Head towards the National Gallery.

Locate the "Fourth Plinth." Some kind of statue or sculpture usually stands atop a "plinth." That was the original plan for this one too, but city planners went back and forth for well over 100 years, and the Fourth Plinth stood vacant.

The planners changed course completely and instead of a British historical figure, today changing modern art displays occupy this prime spot. Until 2014 a huge blue rooster looked down over the square, with future plans for a bronze horse and then a "thumbs up."

☐ **WHAT CURRENTLY OCCUPIES THE "FOURTH PLINTH?"**

☐ **TRACK DOWN THE IMPERIAL MEASUREMENT MARKERS.**

Hint: They're close to the busts of British military heroes near the fountain.

Which do you prefer: metric (meter, centimeter, millimeter) or imperial (yard, foot, inch)?

☐ **HUNT DOWN LONDON'S SMALLEST POLICE STATION.**

2 POINTS

Some say this phone-booth looking structure holds the honor of the world's smallest police station (although others say the title belongs to another booth-like structure standing in a town in Florida). London police originally set up a station here as a lookout point to monitor protests and large crowds gathering in the square. The station even had a direct phone line to Scotland Yard, the city's famous police service. Today this high tech structure merely serves as a storage unit.

☐ **FIND "THE NOSE."**

2 POINTS

Make your way to the Admiralty Arch just off the square. Somewhere on the arch's walls rests a nose sculpture. Some say it's a model of Napoleon's nose (a French emperor who battled the British). According to others, it's a spare nose for Admiral Nelson, while in truth it was left by a daring Brit who decided to affix noses to various landmarks around the city in response to the "nosey" security cameras mounted around the city.

# NATIONAL GALLERY

Hunt down a gift shop for a postcard rack of the museum's works. Together with your case officer, pick out a few postcards of interesting paintings to track down inside. Your case officer sets the number of points per postcard.

POINT(S) EACH

As you explore the museum, stay on point and uncover the below items in paintings. (Examples are included in the images above. However you don't necessarily have to find the paintings provided in the examples.)

☐ SOMEONE ON A HORSE

1 POINT EACH

☐ AN ANGEL

☐ A PERSON HOLDING A BABY

☐ SOMEONE PLAYING AN INSTRUMENT

1 POINT EACH, 8 POINTS MAX

**31+**

**TOTAL POINTS**

- POSTCARDS
- ITEMS IN PAINTINGS
- VAN EYCK
- REMBRANDT
- CRIVELLI
- THE AMBASSADORS
- THREE FAMOUS WORKS
- YOUR FAVORITE PAINTINGS

☐ **TRACK DOWN THE PAINTING WITH THIS MIRROR.**

**2 POINTS**

Hint: The artist's name: Van Eyck. (Van Eyck = "Vahn Ike")

Check out the mirror's details. It reflects the couple in the painting, as well as two others peering in the doorway. One could be the artist himself, a man by the name of "Van Eyck."

☐ **FIND THE "GRAFFITI" DECLARING IN LATIN BASICALLY THAT "JAN VAN EYCK WAS HERE 1434."**

**2 POINTS**

The scroll characters may be a bit hard to decipher, but can you make out the "1", the "3", and the last part of his name?

☐ **HOW MANY CANDLES ARE LIT IN THE CHANDELIER?**

**1 POINT**

● ● ● ● ● ● ● ● ● ● ● ● ● ● ● ● ● ● ● ● ● ● ● ● ● ● ● ● ● ● ● ● ● ● ● ● ● ● ● ● ● ● ● ● ● ● ● ●

☐ **TRACK DOWN THIS MESSAGE.** ● ● ● ● ● ● ● ● ● ● ● ● ● ●

**2 POINTS**

Hint: It's in the painting *Belshazzar's Feast* by Rembrandt.

Here, the hand of God has appeared to deliver a warning to the evil king Belshazzar: his time is up. The artist, however, created the message incorrectly. It's composed in Hebrew, a language written right to left (not left to right, like English), and Rembrandt mistakenly positioned the message in columns.

☐ **LOCATE A PAINTING FILLED WITH BIRDS, INCLUDING A PEACOCK, DOVE, AND ONE IN A CAGE.**

2 ~~TS~~

Hint: The painting is *The Annunciation, with Saint Emidius* by Carlo Crivelli ("Criv-ell-ee").

**UNCOVER:**

☐ **THE ARTIST'S LAST NAME PAINTED IN GOLD**

☐ **SAINT EMIDIUS**

**1** OIN EACH

Hint: He holds a model of the town in the painting (a small village in Italy).

• • • • • • • • • • • • • • • • • • • • • • • • • • • • • • • • • • • • • • • •

☐ **FIND THIS MAN, STANDING PROUDLY IN HIS FUR COAT.**

~~POINTS~~

Hint: The painting title is *The Ambassadors.*

☐ **WHAT IS THE GRAY FIGURE ON THE FLOOR?**

~~POINT~~

Need help? Get close to the painting and stand on the right side to uncover this optical illusion. Some say the artist added this as a reminder that we all die. Others claim the artist wanted this work to hang on a staircase – the perfect angle from which to scare staircase climbers, while some say that he simply added it as a nifty way to impress art collectors with his painting skills.

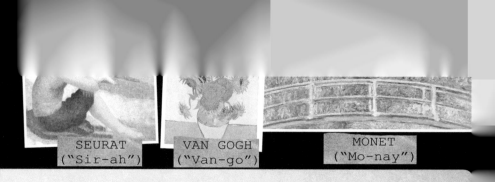

| SEURAT | VAN GOGH | MONET |
|---|---|---|
| ("Sir-ah") | ("Van-go") | ("Mo-nay") |

These images (labelled with the artist's name) are from three of the world's most famous paintings.

☐ **TRACK DOWN THE ORIGINAL PAINTINGS. WHAT ARE THEIR NAMES?**

**2**
POINTS
EACH

*Note: When you find the first one, part of the name, Asnières, is pronounced "Ahn-yair."

☐ **OF ALL THE WORKS IN THE MUSEUM, WHICH ONE(S):**

**3**
POINTS

-DO YOU THINK TOOK THE MOST SKILL TO CREATE?

-WOULD YOU WANT TO ADD TO YOUR COLLECTION IF YOU WERE AN ART COLLECTOR?

my notes:

# BRITISH MUSEUM

ONE OF THE TOP RULES OF SPYING: BLEND IN WITH YOUR SURROUNDINGS. YOU CAN NEVER SPOT THE BEST AGENTS, BECAUSE THEY DON'T LOOK LIKE AGENTS. HERE, THAT MEANS "PLAYING TOURIST" BY STROLLING AROUND THE MUSEUM (AND TAKING A FEW PHOTOS).

Before venturing into the exhibits, stake out the gift shop for a postcard rack of the museum's works. Together with your case officer, pick out a few postcards of interesting items to track down inside. Your case officer sets the number of points per postcard.

**POINT(S) EACH**

☐ FIND THE ROSETTA STONE.

**2 POINTS**

This "decoder" allowed scientists to crack the code on hieroglyphics* and finally understand ancient Egyptian writing.

**31+**

- POSTCARDS
- ROSETTA STONE
- RAMESSES II
- EGYPTIAN ANIMALS
- KATEBET
- SUMERIAN STONE
- PARTHENON MARBLES
- SUTTON HOO BURIAL
- UNUSUAL OBJECTS

**TOTAL POINTS**

*Hieroglyphics = writing that uses characters which resemble pictures

Hieroglyphics

☐ **HUNT DOWN RAMESSES II.** ......................

**2 POINTS**

(one of the most powerful rulers of Ancient Egypt)

In Ancient Egypt, animals held a god-like status.

**FIND:**

☐ **THE FALCON**

**1 POINT**

☐ **THE CAT (ADORNED WITH GOLD JEWELRY)**

**1 POINT**

☐ **THE BEETLE**

**1 POINT**

☐ **LOCATE THE MUMMY OF KATEBET.**

A.k.a. the Chantress of Amun, the King of Gods, this mummy even sports earrings.

☐ **BONUS: HAVE YOUR PHOTO SNAPPED IN A "KATEBET POSE."**

(Stand with your arms crossed around your chest, hands in fists. Extend the index finger of one hand and on the other hand extend your pinky and index finger.)

☐ **IN THE MESOPOTAMIA ROOMS, FIND A STONE WITH "SUMERIAN" SCRIPT.**

The script on this stone, around 5,000 years old, is in the ancient language of Sumerian, a language spoken by people of the land that today is Iraq. It's the world's oldest written language.

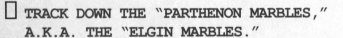

☐ **TRACK DOWN THE "PARTHENON MARBLES," A.K.A. THE "ELGIN MARBLES."**

Not typically what you picture when you hear the word "marbles," these are actually ancient marble sculptures. Dating from around 400 B.C., they show scenes from mythology and were whisked away from Athens' Parthenon temple by a sneaky British ambassador, the Earl of Elgin, in the 1800's.

TRACK DOWN:

☐ **SELENE'S HORSE'S HEAD**

(The horse may appear a bit tired because he just led the chariot of Selene, the Moon goddess, across the sky.)

☐ **THREE GODDESSES**

(Sadly, through the years the three women have lost their heads.)

☐ **BONUS: WHAT ARE THEIR NAMES?**

☐ **CENTAURS**

(Centaurs were half human, half horse. Seven points max.)

The Parthenon

☐ **HUNT DOWN THE SUTTON HOO SHIP BURIAL.**

☐ **BONUS: FIND THIS HELMET, WORN BY AN ENGLISH WARRIOR AROUND 1500 YEARS AGO.**

☐ **WHAT THREE ITEMS IN THE MUSEUM DID YOU FIND THE MOST UNUSUAL?**

1 POINT

1 POINT

1 POINT

1 POINT EACH

2 POINTS

1 POINT

3 POINTS

# BRITISH LIBRARY

SPIES NEED A "COVER": A GO-TO GIG THAT "COVERS" THEIR REAL MISSION. WHILE YOU MAY BE AN AGENT-IN-TRAINING, REMEMBER YOUR "COVER" AS A TOURIST. TIME TO START PLAYING TOURIST BY EXPLORING THIS LOCATION AND UNCOVERING:

## SACRED TEXTS FROM DIFFERENT RELIGIONS

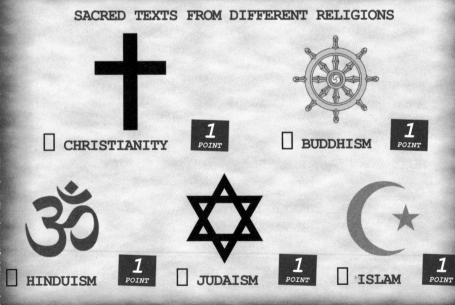

☐ CHRISTIANITY   **1** POINT

☐ BUDDHISM   **1** POINT

☐ HINDUISM   **1** POINT

☐ JUDAISM   **1** POINT

☐ ISLAM   **1** POINT

**17**

**TOTAL POINTS**

## ☐ LOCATE THE MAGNA CARTA.

The *Magna Carta* protected the rights of the citizens against the ever-powerful King of England. Back in these days, kings could do whatever they pleased: their authority was granted by God and they were "above the law." The *Magna Carta* set a limit to the king's power over the people. It declared that the King (King John at the time in 1215) must abide by the laws of the land. For example, the king couldn't simply have one of his subjects locked up just because he pleased. The *Magna Carta* (which means

King John Signing the *Magna Carta*

"Great Charter") became a model for English common law and the U.S. *Constitution* and the *Bill of Rights*.

## ☐ WHO WROTE ALICE IN WONDERLAND (A.K.A. ALICE'S ADVENTURES IN WONDERLAND)?

Hint: Find the original version of this book for the answer.

The Author

## ☐ TRACK DOWN THE DIAMOND SUTRA.

**2 POINTS**

This ancient Buddhist text is one of the world's oldest printed books that's still intact. Back in the 800's (when this text was created) "printing" meant using wooden blocks with ink to create "letters" (the Chinese characters) and pasting paper together.

## ☐ FIND THE TWO LIONS "GUARDING" THE BUDDHA.

**1 POINT**

(Note: These lions may appear more like calm house dogs than the fierce animal known as "king of the jungle.")

## ☐ HUNT DOWN LEONARDO DAVINCI'S NOTEBOOK.

**2 POINTS**

Notice anything strange about the writing on DaVinci's pages? DaVinci, a true genius - an inventor, writer, and painter - wrote the words on these pages with a "mirror" effect. He essentially wrote backwards, right to left (instead of left to right). **Some use mirror writing to encode secret messages. Perhaps DaVinci used it to protect his ideas from prying eyes.**

Leonardo DaVinci

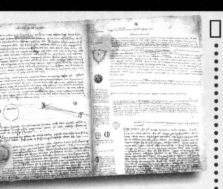

☐ **DECIPHER THE NEXT CLUE, WRITTEN WITH DAVINCI'S MIRROR TECHNIQUE.**

**1 POINT**

**2 POINTS**

Gutenberg

☐ **FIND THE GUTENBERG BIBLE.**

Thanks to Johann Gutenberg, books became available to more and more people in Europe, not just the very rich. He came up with a mechanical way to create books in the 1400's. For the text, Gutenberg created blocks which could be re-used and changed around with different letters and words. Ink was applied, then the blocks were placed on paper again and again - way faster than copying by hand. (Remember though, that the Chinese were producing printed books - like the *Diamond Sutra* - long before this.)

# TEMPLE CHURCH

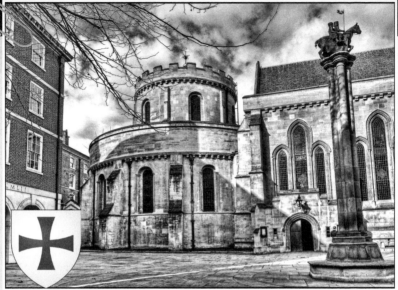

This site served as the English HQ of the Knights Templar, a band of knights that went off to fight in the Crusades, the quest to claim the Holy Lands for Christians and to protect Christian pilgrims visiting this sacred area. Knights' uniforms signified they were part monk (the red cross on a white robe), part professional soldier (the heavy armor). **It was at this very site that they completed top-secret initiation rituals before becoming full-fledged knights and riding off on horseback towards the Holy Land.**

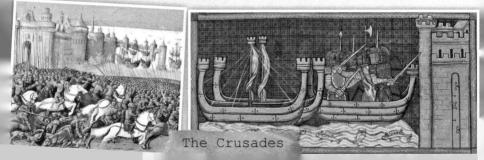

The Crusades

**8**

**TOTAL POINTS**

☐ **FIND THE STATUE OF THE TWO KNIGHTS ON HORSEBACK OUTSIDE THE CHURCH.**

**2 POINTS**

This statue symbolizes the knights' humble beginnings. Before they became wealthy and powerful, the knights rode two to a horse to save money. (That must be one strong horse!)

☐ **TRACK DOWN TWO KNIGHTS WITH THE SAME FIRST AND LAST NAMES, THE FATHER AND SON WITH THE TITLE "EARL OF PEMBROKE."**

**2 POINTS**

Many have given the honor, "history's greatest knight," to the father. Described as "the best friend a king could have," he faithfully served English kings, including Richard the Lionheart.

☐ **LOCATE A STATUE OF A MAN GRIMACING AS HIS EAR GETS BITTEN BY A HUNGRY ANIMAL.**

**2 POINTS**

Once you find these statues, check out the other ones nearby. Examine their expressions – some smile with joy while others frown with anger.

☐ **CHOOSE YOUR FAVORITE AND HAVE YOUR PHOTO SNAPPED STANDING BENEATH IT, IMITATING ITS EXPRESSION.**

**2 POINTS**

# ST. PAUL'S CATHEDRAL

Atop the highest point in London sits St. Paul's Cathedral. For over 1400 years this very spot has seen at least four different "St. Paul's" look out over the city. The one that stands today dates from 1675 – the one before this burned in the Great Fire of London. The fire started in the wee hours of September 2, 1666, in the home of one of the king's bakers. It spread like wildfire thanks to the city's wooden buildings. Miraculously only six people died in the blaze, but thousands were left homeless: over 13,000 houses and 87 churches burned to the ground, including St. Paul's.

Great Fire
of London

**29**

- CITY BUILDINGS
- QUEEN'S STATUE
- ST. PAUL'S WATCH
- THE LIGHT OF THE WORLD
- AMERICAN CHAPEL
- WHISPERING GALLERY
- BIRD'S EYE VIEW
- CRYPT MESSAGE
- WREN TOMB

## *Outside*

**2**
*POINTS*

☐ **UNCOVER THESE CITY BUILDINGS HIDDEN NEAR THE CATHEDRAL'S ENTRANCE.**

They represent Damascus, an ancient city in Syria (a country in the Middle East). The Bible recounts that on the Damascus Road "Saul" was temporarily blinded by a flash of light, heard the words of

Jesus, eventually recovered his sight, became "Paul," and devoted his life to spreading Christianity. The cathedral is named for this man, St. Paul.

**2**
*POINTS*

☐ **FIND THE STATUE HOLDING A BOW, WITH ARROWS SLUNG BEHIND HER BACK, AND HER FOOT RESTING ATOP A POOR MAN'S HEAD.**

This statue represents North America – a land that England was exploring when cathedral construction completed. The statue above honors the Queen of England at that time.

The Queen With Her Son

The Queen With Her Husband

☐ **WHO WAS THE QUEEN?**

**1**
POINT

## *Inside*

☐ **LOCATE THE PLAQUE HONORING ST. PAUL'S WATCH.**

**2**
POINTS

During World War II, London (and Great Britain) came under heavy attack from the Nazis. (Read more about this on page 13.) This plaque reads: "Remember men and women of St. Paul's Watch who by the grace of God saved this cathedral from destruction..."

☐ **TRACK DOWN THIS IMAGE OF JESUS, KNOCKING ON A DOOR WITHOUT A HANDLE.**

**2**
POINTS

In this painting, *The Light of the World*, he knocks and patiently waits at a door that can only be opened from the inside.

Make your way to the American Memorial Chapel. This area of the cathedral was destroyed during World War II and rebuilt to honor the 28,000 Americans who died while serving in the United Kingdom during the war.

☐ **FIND THE GOLDEN BALD EAGLE, A SYMBOL OF THE U.S.**

**4 POINTS**

**SPECIAL AGENTS MUST BE IN TIP-TOP SHAPE, READY TO ESCAPE DANGER AND MAKE A FAST GETAWAY. IT'S TIME TO SEE IF YOU'D MAKE THE CUT.**

**3 POINTS**

☐ **CLIMB THE 250+ STEPS TO THE DOME'S "PIT STOP" VIEWING LEVEL: THE WHISPERING GALLERY.**

Rumor has it that sounds (particularly whispers) travel rather well in this level. Let's put that rumor to the test. Have a teammate stand far away on the other side of the gallery with his/her ear against the wall.

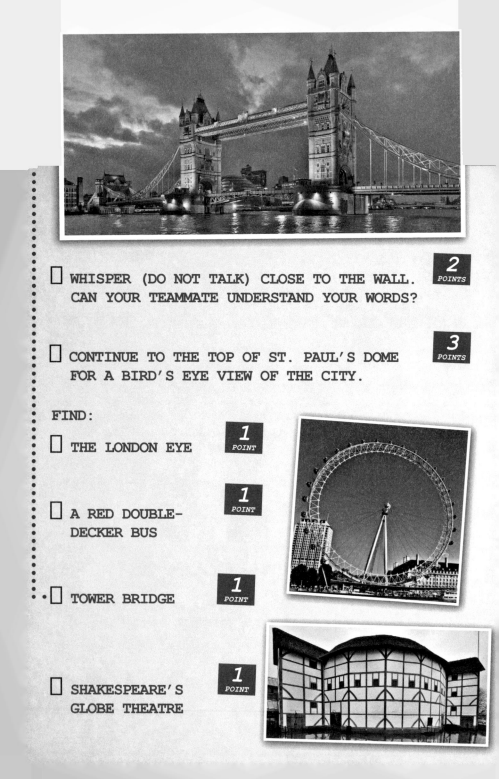

☐ WHISPER (DO NOT TALK) CLOSE TO THE WALL. CAN YOUR TEAMMATE UNDERSTAND YOUR WORDS?

**2 POINTS**

☐ CONTINUE TO THE TOP OF ST. PAUL'S DOME FOR A BIRD'S EYE VIEW OF THE CITY.

**3 POINTS**

FIND:

☐ THE LONDON EYE

**1 POINT**

☐ A RED DOUBLE-DECKER BUS

**1 POINT**

☐ TOWER BRIDGE

**1 POINT**

☐ SHAKESPEARE'S GLOBE THEATRE

**1 POINT**

Admiral Horatio
Nelson

## Crypt

☐ **UNCOVER THE WORDS: "ENGLAND EXPECTS EVERY MAN TO DO HIS DUTY."** **2 POINTS**

This message of the brave British Admiral Horatio Nelson inspired the admiral's sailors at the Battle of Trafalgar, the tragic naval victory that ended in Nelson's death.

☐ **FIND THE TOMB OF SIR CHRISTOPHER WREN, THE CATHE- DRAL'S ARCHITECT.** **2 POINTS**

Sir Christopher Wren

# TOWER OF LONDON

**AGENTS MUST KEEP THEIR COOL AND ACCOMPLISH MISSIONS, EVEN IN NOT-SO-COMFORTABLE SITUATIONS (FOR EXAMPLE, IN OLD CASTLES FILLED WITH MEMORIES OF PRISONERS AND BEHEADINGS). DO YOU HAVE THE STOMACH TO CARRY OUT THIS MISSION DESPITE THE TALES OF DEATH?**

For almost 950 years, the Tower of London has stood watch over the city – serving an array of functions from fortress, prison and zoo, to jewel house and execution site. Back in the tower's heyday, the method of choice for offing prisoners was…beheading.

The Tower has all the makings of a mighty fortress designed to keep enemies out and prisoners in: massive stone walls, wide moats (once filled with water, now grass), and tall lookout towers.

**24**

- DRAWBRIDGE
- ARROW SLITS
- ANIMALS
- WEATHERVANES
- HENRY'S HEAD

- ARMOR
- BEEFEATER
- PRISONER GRAFFITI
- CROWN JEWELS

TOTAL POINTS

☐ **FIND A DRAWBRIDGE.**

**1** POINT

☐ **LOCATE ARROW SLITS.**
   **(FIVE POINTS MAX)**

**1** POINT EACH

(Great for Tower soldiers to shoot arrows from and practically impossible for the enemy to shoot arrows in.)

Keep a lookout for these animals, reminding us of the Tower's previous role as a zoo.

☐ **BEAR** **1** POINT

☐ **LIONS** **1** POINT

☐ **RAVENS** **1** POINT

Legend has it that the Tower of London will remain safe as long as ravens live here. These ravens have had one of their wings clipped, so no safety concerns here.

☐ **FIND FOUR WEATHERVANES LIKE**
   **THESE, TOPPED WITH A CROWN.**

**2** POINTS

These top the castle's famous keep (the castle's strongest tower): White Tower.

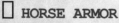
Anne Boleyn

Henry VIII

Catherine Howard

**VENTURE INSIDE THE TOWER AND FIND:**

☐ **THE WOODEN HEAD OF KING HENRY VIII**

**1 POINT**

London has seen beyond its fair share of beheadings. Heads-minus-bodies (like this one) weren't unusual sights around town. Henry VIII (VIII=8) didn't meet his end like this (by beheading), instead he reserved this "honor" for two of his wives. King Henry had six different wives, and two of them, Anne Boleyn and Catherine Howard, were beheaded.

☐ **KING HENRY'S SUIT OF ARMOR**

**1 POINT**

☐ **ARMOR OF THE GIANT AND THE DWARF**

**1 POINT**

(the armor for a 6'8"/two-meter-tall man and that of a midget)

> Hint: These may be displayed together.

☐ **HORSE ARMOR**

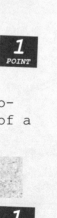
**1 POINT**

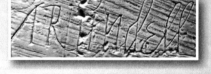

☐ **HAVE YOUR PHOTO TAKEN WITH A "BEEFEATER."**

**2 POINTS**

☐ **BONUS: ASK ONE OF THE GUARDS WHERE THE NAME "BEEFEATER" COMES FROM.**

**2 POINTS**

• • • • • • • • • • • • • • • • • • • • • • • • • • • • • • • • • • • • • • •

Venture to Beauchamp ("Beach-am") Tower, the tower that held VIP prisoners.

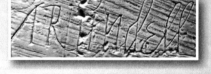

**HUNT DOWN THE PRISONER GRAFFITI ON THE NEXT PAGE.**

The Nine
Days Queen

## ☐ THE DUDLEY "COAT OF ARMS"

1 POINT

The scene: England in the mid-1500's. The sides: Protestants and Catholics, both Christian, and at odds with each other. The Protestants claim the English throne and put Lady Jane Grey, a 15-year-old, a.k.a. the "Nine Days Queen," in power. She serves for only…nine days, then the Catholics take her down. She and her husband, Lord Dudley, get locked up in the Tower of London and await their fate of beheading. This design represents the Dudley family, and some claim the clue below was carved in honor of the Nine Days Queen.

## ☐ THE NAME "JANE"

1 POINT

(The "J" appears like an "I.")

## ☐ THE PERSON KNEELING

1 POINT

Near the Dudley coat of arms, perhaps this person is praying for an (impossible) escape from the Tower.

Locate the royal crown jewels and find:

☐ **ST. EDWARD'S CROWN**

(The crown is worn by newly crowned kings/queens during the ceremony in Westminster Abbey.)

☐ **THE SOVEREIGN'S SCEPTRE**

(In the ceremony the newly crowned king/queen receives this sceptre ("sep-ter") containing the "Great Star of Africa," the world's largest clear cut diamond, weighing in at 530 carats.)

Sceptre

# TOWER BRIDGE

☐ **FIND THE COAT OF ARMS OF THE CITY OF LONDON. (FIVE POINTS MAX)**

**1 POINT EACH**

☐ **BONUS: TRACK DOWN THIS FANCY VERSION OF THE COAT OF ARMS.**

**2 POINTS**

The coat of arms and London's flag both have the red cross of St. George, with the red sword in the upper left background. The sword represents the one that beheaded St. Paul (the patron saint of the city from whom St. Paul's Cathedral gets its name). The translation of the Latin words "Domine Dirige Nos": "Lord Direct Us."

# 15

- COATS OF ARMS X 2
- CHIMNEY
- WALKWAY VIEW

**TOTAL POINTS**

☐ **LOCATE THE TOWER BRIDGE CHIMNEY.**  `2 POINTS`

Hint: It looks like all the other lampposts that line the bridge's sidewalk, but a bit wider and minus the lamp at the top.

This duct connected to a small room under one of the piers where guards once went to escape the cold during London's winters. Smoke from a warming fire would have billowed out of this chimney.

☐ **CROSS THE BRIDGE WALKWAYS, SOARING 138 FEET (42 METERS) ABOVE THE THAMES.**  `2 POINTS`

("Thames" = "Tems")

**FROM THIS WALKWAY (OR FROM THE SIDEWALK) SPOT:**

☐ **THE UK FLAG FLYING SIDE BY SIDE WITH LONDON'S FLAG**  `1 POINT`

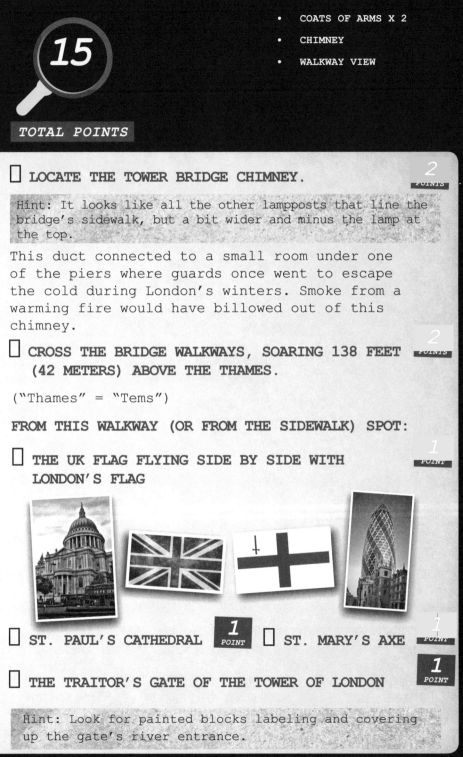

☐ **ST. PAUL'S CATHEDRAL**  `1 POINT`   ☐ **ST. MARY'S AXE**  `1 POINT`

☐ **THE TRAITOR'S GATE OF THE TOWER OF LONDON**  `1 POINT`

Hint: Look for painted blocks labeling and covering up the gate's river entrance.

# HYDE PARK

Marble Arch

Before this landmark welcomed visitors to Hyde Park, the "Marble Arch" stood as a grand gateway to Buckingham Palace, the royal family's HQ. In days past, only royals and members of the military participating in royal ceremonies had the privilege of walking through the arch. Now it's your turn to play "VIP."

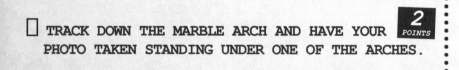

☐ TRACK DOWN THE MARBLE ARCH AND HAVE YOUR **2** POINTS
   PHOTO TAKEN STANDING UNDER ONE OF THE ARCHES.

☐ UNCOVER THESE LIONS ON THE ARCH. **2** POINTS

# 9

**TOTAL POINTS**

- ARCH PHOTO
- ARCH'S LIONS
- HORSE HEAD
- FOUNTAIN
- DIANA'S TITLE

☐ **NEAR THE ARCH, FIND THE HORSE HEAD.**  **2 POINTS**

Trek into the park towards the lake called "The Serpentine" for the rest of this mission.

☐ **UNCOVER AN OVAL-SHAPED FOUNTAIN WITH SECTIONS LIKE THIS.**  **2 POINTS**

This memorial is named in honor of Diana, the UK's beloved princess who died tragically in a car crash in Paris in 1997.

Diana

☐ **DIANA'S OFFICIAL TITLE WAS "PRINCESS OF _____."**  **1 POINT**

Hint: Find the sign on a fence with the memorial's description, or locate her title inscribed on the fountain. The answer is one of the countries that makes up the United Kingdom.

# ANYTIME MISSIONS

**THE BEST AGENTS HAVE A HIGH LEVEL OF SOMETHING CALLED "SITUATIONAL AWARENESS." THESE QUICK-WITTED AGENTS PAY CLOSE ATTENTION TO THEIR SURROUNDINGS — READY TO COLLECT CRITICAL INTELLIGENCE AND RESPOND TO DANGEROUS SITUATIONS. HAVING EXCELLENT "SITUATIONAL AWARENESS" ("SA" FOR SHORT) MEANS ALWAYS BEING "ON POINT."**

## *BRITISH SYMBOLS*

**AS YOU TREK AROUND THE CITY AND ITS MONUMENTS, REMAIN ON ALERT FOR THESE TO EARN UP TO FIFTEEN POINTS MAX.**

☐ **THREE LIONS CREST:**

Richard the Lionheart adopted three gold lions as a symbol of England in the 1100's during the Crusades.

☐ **ROYAL COAT OF ARMS**

☐ **TUDOR ROSE, A.K.A. THE ROSE OF ENGLAND:**

This rose gets its name from the Tudor Dynasty, the royal Tudor family who ruled England and Ireland from the late 1400's to the early 1600's.

**☐ RED TELEPHONE BOX:**

**1 POINT EACH**

To earn this point, you must have your photo snapped pretending to make a call from inside.

*FOOD*

**TRY THESE NATIONAL FOODS OF GREAT BRITAIN:**

**☐ FISH AND CHIPS**

**1 POINT**

Deep-fried fish with fried potatoes (similar to French fries) topped off with vinegar.

**☐ TEA**

**1 POINT**

Sight-seeing making you sleepy? Get a jolt of caffeine as you enjoy England's beverage of choice.

Try the ultimate snack with your tea: scones (similar to biscuits), jam, and clotted cream (a cross between whipped cream and butter).

**☐ CURRY**

**1 POINT**

There are many types of curry, but the one voted England's favorite, "Chicken Tikka Masala," has its roots from Indian cooking. It has a smooth, spicy sauce, usually made from cream and tomatoes.

*LONDON SOCCER*

HUNT DOWN JERSEYS FOR SOME OF LONDON'S PREMIER LEAGUE SOCCER* TEAMS.

☐ ARSENAL **1** POINT

☐ CHELSEA **1** POINT

☐ CRYSTAL PALACE **1** POINT

☐ QUEEN'S PARK RANGERS **1** POINT

☐ TOTTENHAM **1** POINT

☐ WEST HAM UNITED **1** POINT

*Soccer is called "football" in the UK.

# ANYTIME MISSIONS: BONUS

COME ACROSS A MONUMENT OR EXHIBIT THAT'S CLOSED? NOT ENOUGH TIME IN LONDON? HAVE NO FEAR, USE THESE MISSIONS TO ACHIEVE YOUR GOAL. YOUR CASE OFFICER SETS THE POINTS.

POINT(S) PER ROUTE ☐ TOGETHER WITH YOUR CASE OFFICER, PLAN YOUR ROUTES IN THE "TUBE," A.K.A. THE "UNDERGROUND," LONDON'S SUBWAY SYSTEM.

POINT(S) ☐ HEAR A TUBE ANNOUNCER WARNING PASSENGERS TO "MIND THE GAP."

This announcement tells passengers to be careful as they cross the gap between the train door and the platform.

London is a multi-cultural city full of residents and tourists from all over the world. Listen up for people speaking languages other than English.

POINT(S) ☐ FOR EVERY FOREIGN LANGUAGE YOU AND YOUR CASE OFFICER CAN IDENTIFY.

POINT(S) ☐ COUNT HOW MANY CAPSULES SPIN AROUND ON THE LONDON EYE - THE GIANT OBSERVATION WHEEL.

# ANSWER KEY

Once an answer is submitted, your case officer can check it here. If you peek at this answer key before submitting a final answer, you won't receive any points for that clue. Most clues do not have one correct answer, for those that do, here are the answers.

**#1 Westminster Abbey:**
-The skeleton has a dart/an arrow.
-The soldier was buried on Nov 11, 1920.
-Lions support the Coronation Chair.
-As of 2014, the most recent royal to be crowned was Queen Elizabeth II.
-Newton's elbow rests on books.
-Shakespeare's finger is pointing to the word "temples." Three books rest below his elbow.

**#2 Houses of Parliament/Big Ben:** The statue is Oliver Cromwell.

**#3 Buckingham Palace:** The queen: Victoria. Three children are with her.

**#4 Trafalgar Square:** Nelson lost his right arm. The president is George Washington.

**#5 National Gallery:**
-In the chandelier, one candle is lit.
-On the floor there's a skull.
-The three paintings: *The Bathers at Asnières*, *Sunflowers*, and *The Water Lily Pond*.

**#6 British Museum:** The three goddesses are: Hestia, Dione and Aphrodite.

**#7 British Library:** Lewis Carroll/ Charles Dodgson wrote *Alice in Wonderland*.

**#9 St. Paul's Cathedral:** The queen: Anne.

**#12 Hyde Park:** Diana's title was "Princess of Wales."

**#13 Anytime Missions Bonus:** The London Eye has 32 capsules.

Note: the information in this book was accurate as of October 2014. We hope that you won't find anything outdated related to the clues.

If you do find that something has changed, please email us at info@ScavengerHuntAdventures.com to kindly let us know.

## THE FINAL MISSION

Case officers, please visit
**scavengerhuntadventures.com/bonus**
(all lowercase letters)

☐ **JOIN 'THE INSIDER' (OUR EMAIL LIST)**
You'll get a special bonus mission for
this city plus our free e-book,
*The Museum Spy*.

"I'm Joining
Today!"

## PLEASE HELP SPREAD THE WORD

We're a small family business and would be
thrilled if you **left a review online*** or
**recommended our books to a friend**.

"We'd Love
To Help!"

Our books: Paris, London, Amsterdam, Rome, NYC, D.C.,
Barcelona, Florence, St. Augustine, with more coming!

*We can't mention the site name here, but it begins with "AM"!

## A BIG THANK YOU

Thank you for supporting
our family-owned business.

Mom writes, Dad serves in the military, and
Jr. helps "research" our books. **Without
you this series wouldn't be possible.**

Thank <u>YOU</u>!

*Catherine*

by A1C Harry Brexel

**www.ScavengerHuntAdventures.com**